Book by
Marcia Milgrom Dodge
& Anthony Dodge

Additional Material by
Rob Bartlett, Lynne Taylor-Corbett
& Sharon Vaughn

Songs by
Doug Besterman, Susan Birkenhead,
Michele Brourman, Pat Bunch,
Gretchen Cryer, Anthony Dodge, Marcia
Milgrom Dodge, Beth Falcone,
David Friedman, Kathie Lee Gifford, David
Goldsmith, Carol Hall, Henry Krieger,
Stephen Lawrence, Melissa Manchester,
Amanda McBroom, Pam Tillis &
Sharon Vaughn

A SAMUEL FRENCH ACTING EDITION

SAMUEL FRENCH
FOUNDED 1830
NEW YORK HOLLYWOOD LONDON TORONTO

SAMUELFRENCH.COM

IMPORTANT BILLING AND CREDIT
REQUIREMENTS

All producers of *HATS!* *must* give credit to the Author of the Play in all programs distributed in connection with performances of the Play, and in all instances in which the title of the Play appears for the purposes of advertising, publicizing or otherwise exploiting the Play and/or a production. The name of the Author *must* appear on a separate line on which no other name appears, immediately following the title and *must* appear in size of type not less than fifty percent of the size of the title type.

(Name of Producer presents)
"HATS!"
Book by Marcia Milgrom Dodge and Anthony Dodge

"Inspired by the stories, experiences and mission of "
(insert logo of Red Hat Society)

Songs by Doug Besterman, Susan Birkenhead, Michele Brourman, Pat Bunch, Gretchen Cryer, Anthony Dodge, Marcia Milgrom Dodge, Beth Falcone, David Friedman, Kathie Lee Gifford, David Goldsmith, Carol Hall, Henry Krieger, Stephen Lawrence, Melissa Manchester, Amanda McBroom, Pam Tillis & Sharon Vaughn

Additional Material by Rob Barlett, Lynne Taylor-Corbett and Sharon Vaughn

"Special Thanks to Maxine Philippe – "Lady Maxx"

"Conceived by Mitchell Maxwell"

"HATS!" was originally produced at the New Denver Civic Theatre by Sibling Theatricals, Inc. and is presented by arrangement with Hats Holdings, LLC and Sibling Theatricals, Inc. in New York City

(1) After the billing of all composers and authors, any contributing writers must be credited under the tag: "Additional Material by Rob Barlett, Lynne Taylor-Corbett and Sharon Vaughn"

(2) The Red Hat Society shall be granted a biography describing the organization of the Red Hat Society including text providing information to become a member of the Red Hat Society.

(3) Sibling Theatricals, Inc. shall be granted a biography describing the organization including text that states that the Original Cast Album was produced by Sibling Music Corp.

(4) A biography shall appear for each of the author(s), composer(s), or other artistic personnel for artistic material or services arranged by the Agent for the presentation of the Play in the Territory.

(5) A copy of each program created for the venue where the Play is presented by the Licensee in the Territory shall be submitted to Hats Holdings, Inc. prior to the final performance of the Play.

THE NEW DENVER CIVIC THEATRE

A Sibling Theatricals, Inc. Production

Book by

Marcia Milgrom Dodge and Anthony Dodge

Inspired by the stories, experiences and mission of the

Songs by

Doug Besterman, Susan Birkenhead, Michele Brourman, Pat Bunch, Gretchen Cryer, Anthony Dodge, Marcia Milgrom Dodge, Beth Falcone, David Friedman, Kathie Lee Gifford, David Goldsmith, Carol Hall, Henry Krieger, Stephen Lawrence, Melissa Manchester, Amanda McBroom, Pam Tillis & Sharon Vaughn

Additional Material by
Rob Bartlett

Starring

Leslie Alexander, Miche Braden, Susan Long, Nora Mae Lyng,
Pamela Myers, Teri Ralston, Cheryl Stern

Scenery Designer **Narelle Sissons**	*Costume Designer* **Judanna Lynn**	*Lighting Designer* **Jason Kantrowitz**	*Sound Designer* **Ben Neafus**

Puppet Designer   *Music, Vocal & Dance Arrangements*
Eric Wright   **Doug Besterman & Steven M. Alper**

Orchestrations by   *Music Director*
Larry Blank and Peter Myers   **Steven M. Alper**

National Press Representative   *Casting*
Keith Sherman Associates   **Carol Hanzel Casting**
Cindi Rush Casting, Ltd.

Denver Press Representatives   *Marketing*
Webb PR   **Karen Meyer**

General Management   *Production Stage Manager*   *Production Manager*
Brent Peek Productions   **A. Phoebe Sacks**   **Benjamin Neafus**

Special Thanks to Maxine Phillippe – "Lady Maxx"
Musical Supervision by
Doug Besterman

Directed and Choreographed by
Lynne Taylor-Corbett

SIBLING
THEATRICALS, INC

CHARACTERS

(in order of appearance)

LADY - Mid-to-late 70s. **MARYANNE**'s mother. Widow and loving grand-mother.

BARONESS - Age 52. Divorcee. Corporate success. Affluent. From Texas.

CONTESSA - Late 50s. Hispanic. Packed with attitude and a tendency to exaggerate. Married.

DAME - Mid-50s. An empty-nester. Wife adn mother of three.

DUCHESS - 65. African-American. Big-boned with sass and ego. Great marriage.

PRINCESS - Late 50s-to-early 60s. Breast cancer survivor. Divorcee. Absent-minded and forever optimistic.

MARYANNE - 49.999. Teacher. Married. Struggling with her impending 50th birthday.

MUSICAL INTRODUCTION

(As the Overtur-ette finishes, five specials come up across the front of the stage revealing **LADY, BARONESS, CONTESSA, DAME, DUCHESS** *and* **PRINCESS**. *Each of the women stand, dressed in their finest attire, sporting a stunning red hat and holding a birthday present. They sing:)*

SONG: FIFTY
Lyrics by Susan Birkenhead, Music by Henry Krieger

LADY.
> WHEN I WAS A KID
> FIFTY WAS ELDERLY

BARONESS.
> OVER THE HILL,
> WRINKLED AND GREY

LADY.
> FIFTY WAS "MOM,
> YOU NO LONGER MATTER

CONTESSA.
> FIFTY WAS FADED
> FIFTY WAS FATTER!

DAME.
> FIFTY,
> THAT WAS MY GRANDMOTHER
> WHOM I WILL SOMEDAY BE…

DUCHESS.
> GROW OLD GRACEFULLY?
> SURE, I WILL…

ALL.
> BUT NOT TILL I'M NINETY-THREE!!!

(There is a huge lighting shift. The stage explodes with color. The women start into a beautifully choreographed number in which they set up for a birthday party.)

WE'RE FIFTY,
OR SIXTY
OR EIGHTY
OR PLUS!
THE WORLD IS OUR PLAYGROUND
THE PARTY IS US!

WE FEEL GOOD,
WE LOOK GOOD,
WE LOVE WHERE WE'VE BEEN,
WE'RE FIFTY,
YEAH, FIFTY,
LET THE GOOD TIMES BEGIN!

BARONESS.

TWENTY WAS PARTIES
AND MAKEUP
AND BOYS.

DAME.

THIRTY
WAS LAUNDRY
AND PLAYDATES
AND NOISE.

DUCHESS.

FORTY
WAS CHAOS,
A HOUSEFUL
OF TEENS.

ALL.

SO WHO HAD TIME
TO FIGURE OUT
WHAT WOMANHOOD MEANS?

BUT NOW WE'RE...
FIFTY!
WE'RE FIFTY
YOUNG GIRLS NO MORE!

WE'RE OLDER
WE'RE WISER
THAN WE WERE BEFORE!

WE FEEL GOOD,
WE LOOK GOOD
WE LOVE WHERE WE'VE BEEN
BECAUSE WE'RE FIFTY!
YEAH, FIFTY!
LET THE GOOD TIMES BEGIN...

(LADY looks at her watch. They set a beautiful hatbox on a pedestal.)

LADY. Hurry! Hurry! Hurry! I don't want her to expect anything!

DUCHESS. Where is she?

LADY. Downstairs. Hurry or she'll start to get suspicious.

PRINCESS. Alright ladies: stack the presents! Light the candles! Fix your hats! Dim the lights!

DAME. When did G.I. Geriatric get here?

PRINCESS. I heard that!

DAME. I'm only teasing.

LADY. *(to PRINCESS)* Just remember this was YOUR idea! I promised MaryAnne – no surprises.

PRINCESS. Why not?! Everyone loves a surprise! And besides – birthdays are just nature's way of telling us to eat more cake!

GIRLS.
WE'RE FIFTY
YOU HEARD US
FIFTY !
FIVE OH!
WE'RE READY TO SHOUT IT
LET EVERYONE KNOW!

WE FEEL GOOD,
WE LOOK GOOD,
WE LOVE WHERE WE'VE BEEN
BECAUSE WE'RE FIFTY!

YEAH, FIFTY!

LET THE GOOD TIMES...

LADY. Alright – everyone hide! I'm gonna go get her!

*(**LADY** runs offstage to get **MARYANNE**. The other women rush to find hiding places as they softly sing:)*

GIRLS.

WE'RE FIFTY...

WE'RE FIFTY...

WE'RE FIFTY...

WE'RE FIFTY...

LET THE GOOD TIMES...

*(**MARYANNE** enters with **LADY** as the women vault out of their hiding spots.)*

LADY. Surprise!!!

GIRLS.

BEGIN!!!!

PLAYOFF MUSIC

(The song ends with a bang. The girls laugh and adlib.)

MARYANNE. What – what's all this?

PRINCESS. Did you think we'd forget?! Did you think we'd let your birthday pass you by unnoticed? Your fif –

MARYANNE. Don't! Don't even say the word!

PRINCESS. What? Fifty?

MARYANNE. Oh God! It sounds so aaaaawwwwffff uuuuulllllll!!! And besides, I don't turn...you know... for quite some time. I still have *(refers to watch)* a good... seventy-four minutes and 18 seconds to go. So I am NOT FIFTY!

*(**MARYANNE** has a mini-breakdown.)*

LADY. Girls – why don't you give us a second.

*(The girls exit. As they do, **MARYANNE** sulks to the table and picks up one of the birthday cards. She reads it:)*

MARYANNE.

"To my Daughter Dear on her Birthday:
  Here are words of simple truth,
    Easy to say yet cleverly sage.
      If forty is the old age of Youth;
        Then fifty's the Youth of Old Age!"
…Adorable.

LADY. Maryanne, what's wrong with you?

MARYANNE. I don't know…maybe the whole surprise party with the menopausal pep squad –

LADY. Maryanne! That's not very nice – true – but not nice.

MARYANNE. *(addresses the audience)* I'm sorry! I'm sorry! Really I am. I don't want to seem like an ingrate, I really do appreciate the effort and all. They are all perfectly well-meaning, OLDER women. *(back to* **LADY***)* But I have nothing in common with them – and I really don't want to. I mean "fifty!" Middle-aged. Middle-aged if you live to be 100!

LADY. Maryanne –

MARYANNE. Tell me this isn't happening. Please.

LADY. Don't you think you're overreacting just a touch?

MARYANNE. No.

LADY. MaryAnne, you're impossible! Let me get the girls. You'll see. *(She exits.)*

MARYANNE. *(calling after her)* No. Yes. Maybe. I don't know? I mean, I'll admit…

SONG: I DON'T WANT
Lyrics by Kathie Lee Gifford, Music by David Friedman
(BELL TONE…)

MARYANNE.

LIFE SO FAR HAS BEEN GOOD TO ME
I HAVE VERY LITTLE REGRETS
I SAVED UP FOR THAT RAINY DAY COMING
BUT I WASN'T EXPECTING TO GET WET YET.

SO IT COMES AS QUITE A SHOCK TO ME
AFTER BEING A GREAT MOTHER AND WIFE
THAT I FIND MYSELF SOMEHOW, *HERE*
ON THE OTHER SIDE OF MY LIFE

(spoken) "I just thought it would take so much longer
to get here, you know?"

I DON'T WANT TO BE SOMEBODY ELSE
I JUST WANT TO BE A YOUNGER ME
HAVE PEOPLE CONFUSE ME WITH SOMEBODY ELSE
LIKE, SAY…ANGELINA JOLIE

I DON'T WANT WHAT I'VE NEVER HAD
I JUST WANT WHAT I HAD BEFORE
FIRM BREASTS, TIGHT THIGHS, AND UNLINED EYES
GOD KNOWS I'M NOT ASKING FOR MORE

(spoken) "All right, I am!"

I DON'T WANT TO SEE MY MOTHER WHEN I SEE MY
OWN FACE
DON'T WANT TO SEE NEW HAIRS IN A BRAND NEW
PLACE
DON'T WANT COTTAGE CHEESE EXCEPT ON MY
PLATE
AND WHEN I STARVE MYSELF ON COTTAGE CHEESE,
I WANT TO LOSE WEIGHT!

AND SPEAKING OF LOSING, I DON'T WANT TO LOSE
MY MIND
DON'T CARE TO LOSE MY HEARING, NOT TOO KEEN
ON GOING BLIND
I DON'T WANT BUNIONS AS BIG AS MY FEET
OR VARICOSE VEINS AS LONG AS MY STREET
OR CATARACTS OR LIVER SPOTS OR PAIN OR HOT
FLASHES
STRETCH MARKS, INSOMNIA, OR SUDDEN
MUSTACHES
DON'T WANT TO WAKE UP IN A RIVER OF SWEAT
I AIN'T A SPRING CHICKEN BUT THIS DUCK AIN'T
DEAD YET!

(spoken) "You want a list?"

I DON'T WANT TO BE: AGGRAVATED, AGITATED,
OBLIGATED, EXASPERATED, UNDERATED,
MANIPULATED,
INTIMIDATED, DEPRICATED, DOMINATED,
DILAPIDATED,
DENIGRATED, CONSTIPATED!

(The girls sneak back onstage.)

BUT ONCE IN A WHILE, I ADMIT
I WOULDN'T MIND ONE LITTLE BIT
BEING MEDICATED OR INTOXICATED

(spoken) "Truth be told, I wouldn't mind being stimulated and penetrated, but hell, for that I'd need to be *lubricated*!"

I DON'T NEED SOME DAMN DOCTOR'S DIAGNOSIS.
I *NEED* A *HUMP* THAT DON'T COME FROM
OSTEOPOROSIS!!!!

LADY. Maryanne!!!

MARYANNE.

I LOVE LIFE AND I WANT TO KEEP GOING
WITHOUT ALL THE YEARS OF EXPERIENCE SHOWING
I GUESS IT'S PRETTY EASY TO SEE
I DON'T WANT TO BE OLDER

I JUST WANT TO BE THE OLD ME

(spoken) Is that too much to ask?

LADY. No. It's not. I understand just the way you're feeling –

THE GIRLS. We all do! We do, Maryanne! Really we do…ad lib…etc.

PRINCESS. But turning fifty isn't so bad –

DAME. Especially when you consider the alternative.

MARYANNE. Oh God!

PRINCESS. That's not what I meant!

LADY. Will you two cut it out. Listen, honey – we've all been there.

DAME. It's true.

DUCHESS & CONTESSA. We have.

(There is a lighting shift and we see **DUCHESS** *and* **CONTESSA** *move into specials downstage right and left. They speak out to the audience.)*

DUCHESS DEE-LOVELY & CONTESSA CONFESSA

DUCHESS. 1943 brought American troops across the Mediterranean to Sicily, race riots in Detroit and Harlem, A Tree Grew in Brooklyn while a Surrey With a Fringe On Top arrived from Oklahoma. A new music swept the country called Jive bringing its terpsichorean baby, The Jitterbug, and last but certainly not least, 1943 brought the arrival of – Me!

*(***CONTESSA** *enters pushing a vanity. During the scene, she sits and sews feathers on her red hat.)*

CONTESSA. Can I tell you something? My friends have given me the Royal name La Contessa Confessa. But I don't get it; I mean what does that mean? So OK, by the way, I am 57 years old, and I wear size 8. OK, I mean I will wear a size 8 when I finish my diet – next month. I only have about 2 sizes to go. OK, 3.

DUCHESS. You see before you Duchess DeLovely, a happy woman of 63, with most of my original parts, all of my original husband, five grown children, several assorted sons and daughters-in-law, and six of the world's best grandkids...I even have a "grand-son-in-law" – but let's not bring up that fool. My Mama always said to me: "Girl, if you don't have anything nice to say about someone, then don't tell your daddy, cause that man will repeat most anything."

CONTESSA. I have been happily married to the same man for – 29 years. OK, but there was a break in the middle there when I was married to husband numero dos for three years – but when Dos started smacking me around *(blows)* Adios Dos! So, I guess you could say I was married for 11 years plus another 18 years, with a little coffee break in between.

DUCHESS. I've been a housewife, a mother, a best friend, chief cook and bottle washer. I've worked part-time, full-time, at home, for someone, with someone and all on my own.

CONTESSA. I've been a housewife, a mother, doctor, lawyer, Indian Chief. As Mama would say: Mucho trabajo, poco dinero – "Lotsa work, little money!" As my husband would say – OK, that's husband one and three, not the coffee break – he'd say: Little money but a lot of laughs. *(laughing, then – not)* OK, that's why I divorced his ass that first time.

DUCHESS. Last week my husband and I were out for Sunday brunch when I noticed he was looking over my shoulder, smiling at these women sittin' behind me. Now he ain't never done that before. I mean, why he got to look around when he's got all this? I was two seconds off of takin' off my shoe and knockin' him upside the head. Then I noticed that the women were all around my age – wearin' fantastic hats and just havin' themselves a good ol' time.

CONTESSA. A little bit ago my husband and I were on a weekend getaway. See, he decided to spend money on me so I decided to keep him this time. At our hotel there was a whole group of women in crazy hats who were at least my age and they were laughing like I do, after two frozen margaritas, okay four...*(holding up 5 fingers)*

DUCHESS. So, I went over and asked them if they were a club.

CONTESSA. So I said, OK, what's the deal with all the hats?

DUCHESS. I had on a hat too – we were dressed for church.

CONTESSA. I had on a cute baseball cap with rhinestones that spell out *CALIENTE.*

DUCHESS. The Girls complimented it and asked...

CONTESSA & DUCHESS. ...if it came in red!

CONTESSA. They said that they were part of a club...

(They begin finishing each other's sentences.)

DUCHESS. ...whose official sport was shopping...

CONTESSA. ...and I said...

CONTESSA & DUCHESS. I'm in!

CONTESSA. And just like that, I felt like a kid again! *(puts on her feathered hat)* You like, eh? I made it myself. Ladies, I've reached the stage in life where I...Ladies, I've reached the stage in life where I...*(She grabs a sparkly belt and wraps it around her waist. It won't close.)* where I... no longer like this belt! *(She throws the belt away.)* Dios mio! Remember how excited we were to grow up? We couldn't wait to sneak out of the house. We couldn't wait to buy our first tampon.

SONG: CINCO PASOS DE LA VIDA
Music & Lyrics by Melissa Manchester and Sharon Vaughn

CONTESSA.
WE COULDN'T WAIT TO IRON OUR HAIR,
LEARN TO KISS AND SMOKE AND SWEAR,
STUFF KLEENEX IN OUR FIRST BRASSIERE
DOUBLE A CUP
(BOOM A BOOM BOOM)

THE FRIEND WHO CAME AND STAINED OUR PANTS
STAYED FOR DAYS AND GAVE US CRAMPS,
BLED HALF TO DEATH WHEN WE SHAVED OUR LEGS.
WE WERE GROWING UP.

WE LIVED ON MOVIE MAGAZINES,
SWEATERS TIGHT AND TIGHTER JEANS,
AND FELL FOR GUYS THAT HAD JAMES DEAN'S
SEXY LITTLE POUT.

CONTESSA/DAME/BARONESS.
SOME OF US WERE A LITTLE TOO FREE

CONTESSA.
AND LEARNED WHAT TROUBLE MEN COULD BE

ALL.
WENT FROM AN "A"-CUP TO SIZE "DOUBLE-D"

CONTESSA.

WE WERE FILLING OUT.

DAME/BARONESS.

LA LA LA LA LA LA LA

FIVE STAGES OF A   DOO DOO

WOMAN'S LIFE,   DOO DOO

FROM PLAYING HOUSE TO

SOMEONE'S WIFE TWICE!

ALL.

CINCO PASOS DE LA VIDA.

LA LA LA LA LA LA LA

FIVE STAGES OF A WOMAN'S LIFE,

CONTESSA.

WE'RE LEARNING TO SURVIVE

ALL.

CINCO PASOS DE LA VIDA

CONTESSA.

THEN WE HAD CHILDREN BLESS-ED BE

I HAD THEM, NOW THEY HAVE ME,

WE GIVE UP MONEY, SEX AND SLEEP

THEN BOOM!

ALL.

EVERYTHING'S ROUND!

PILATES YOGA CABBAGE SOUP,

ATKINS, SOUTH BEACH, WE WERE DUPED.

CONTESSA.

TO BE A SIX WE'D JUMP THROUGH HOOPS

ALL.

GOT TO SLIM DOWN.

CONTESSA.

JUST WHEN WE SHOULD BE HITTING OUR PEAKS

HERE COME THE WRINKLES

ALL.

ON ALL FOUR CHEEKS

BULGES APPEAR WHERE BONES USED TO BE

WE WERE FREAKIN' OUT!

CONTESSA. Excuse me. *(begins having a panic attack)*

DAME & BARONESS. Uno: Growing up

Dos: Filling out

Tres: Holding it in

Quatro: Freaking out!

Cinco:

CONTESSA.

THE HELL WITH IT!!!

ALL.

LA LA LA LA LA LA LA

FIVE STAGES OF A WOMAN'S LIFE,

CONTESSA.

HORIZONTAL TO VERTICAL STRIPES

ALL.

CINCO PASOS DE LA VIDA.

CONTESSA.

EVERYBODY!!

*(**LADY, DUCHESS** and **PRINCESS** with maracas cross behind them from stage left.)*

CONTRESSA/DAME/BARONESS.

FIVE STAGES OF A WOMAN'S LIFE,

FROM PLAYING HOUSE TO SOMEONE'S WIFE. TWICE!!

CINCO PASOS DE LA VIDA.

ALL WOMEN.

LA LA LA LA LA LA LA

(Maraca women exit stage right.)

CONTESSA/DAME/BARONESS.

FIVE STAGES OF A WOMAN'S LIFE,

HOW THE HELL DID WE SURVIVE?

CINCO PASOS DE LA VIDA.

DAME.

IT'S A FAIT A COMPLITA.

CONTESSA.

I THINK IT BEARS A REPEATA.

BARONESS.

I THINK I NEED A FAJITA

CONTESSA.

AND MAYBE ONE MORE MARGARITA.

ALL.

CINCO PASOS DE LA VIDA

AY-AY-AY!

PLAYOFF MUSIC
(Maraca women cross back to stage right followed by **PRINCESS***)*

PRINCESS.

AY-AY-AY!

MARYANNE. *(caught up in the dance)* AY-AY-AY! Who knew that turning "fifty" came with a floor show?!

BARONESS. I know! Don't you just love that Contessa Confessa?

MARYANNE. Yeah, she's great. Contessa Confessa! But does anybody have a normal name around here? Contessa, Duchess…

PRINCESS. We all have regular names, MaryAnne, but when we get together we like to get all dolled up and for a little while we get be whatever we want to be. Besides, would you rather be a commoner, or – *(strikes a regal pose)* – "royalty?"

MARYANNE. Good point. *(singing)* Yeah, great – five stages of a woman's life. Well, you know what? I'm not ready for "to hell with it."

PRINCESS. *(to the audience)* I think MaryAnne needs a little encouragement. *(encourages audience to applaud)*

MARYANNE. This is embarrassing…please stop!

PRINCESS. *(to* **BARONESS***)* You tell her! This was YOU two years ago. *(***PRINCESS*** exits).*

BARONESS. Ha! Ha! I know how you feel; I use to be shy. If you get nervous, just do what I do – *(Blackberry beeps, vibrates and cuts her off. She sighs as if in pleasure.)* Excuse me. I LOVE this thing. It listens, it takes messages and it vibrates! Mitch always hated it. Reminded him that I was a little higher up on the corporate food chain than he was. I never realized that it bothered him so much but I guess it did. When he left me, I thought it was the end of the world. Oh, it wasn't the money. I was pretty well off financially. I didn't need to keep working so hard. So, of course I worked even harder.

See, I didn't really like coming home to my tastefully decorated and suddenly very empty condo, so I took projects by the briefcaseful. I did spreadsheets, online projections and excelled at Excel. I traveled for the firm every chance I got including up the almighty corporate ladder.

My buddy Anita, she kept telling me I should get over myself, be a girl, go buy a hat and find a new man. She'd call me and blab and I'd listen while I defrosted a Lean Cuisine in the microwave and multitasked on my PowerBook. She of course thought it was just what I needed and I, of course, thought it was just a little too precious.

So I was on a conference trip to Scottsdale, and I was in the gift shop when I saw this really awesome red cowboy hat. On the spur of the moment, I slapped down my MasterCard and I took that sucker home. Then I chickened out and stuck it in the closet.

But I couldn't forget it.

In business I am successful because I am fearless, but here was something that scared the hell out of me, and it was just a silly cowboy hat. It was the idea that scared me, the idea of taking time out just for me. Fun with no agenda – terrifying.

And then – I turned fifty! Shit! I don't know how it happened, and I don't know where the time went. But suddenly I was divorced, stressed-out, and 50 with a capital F.

Now Anita? She had already made it to 52 and handled

it so easily. So we're at lunch at my club and I asked her, "What is your secret?" And this woman that I have known since we were in college looked at me and said, "Honey, age doesn't matter unless you're a cheese." I laughed so hard I nearly wet myself. *(pause)* Okay, I did.

And when I went home I went straight to that closet, I took out that hat and I put it on. I still work hard, "Have Blackberry, Will Travel." But when I put on my beautiful cow*girl* hat, I have fun with a capital F.

SONG: THE OLDER THE FIDDLE, THE SWEETER THE TUNE!
Lyrics by Pam Tillis and Pat Bunch, Music by Pam Tillis

BARONESS.
I'M A VINTAGE WINE, CLASSIC DESIGN.
THESE AREN'T WRINKLES, THEY'RE MY PATINA.
I'M A WOMAN OF A CERTAIN AGE.
AND YOU KNOW WHAT I MEAN-A.
I'M A BOOK THAT'S 'BOUT TO GET TO THE GOOD PART.
I'M A ROSE IN SECOND BLOOM.
AND THE OLDER THE FIDDLE
THE SWEETER THE TUNE.

WHEN YOU'RE A FRESH FACED PRODIGY
YOUR PLAYING MAY BE NIFTY.
BUT YOU DON'T REALLY KNOW THE SCORE
UNTIL YOU'RE OVER FIFTY.
AND IF I JUST REPEAT AND FADE
I'D BE HANGIN' UP MY BOW TOO SOON.

*(**DAME** enters.)*

BARONESS/DAME.
'CAUSE THE OLDER THE FIDDLE
THE SWEETER THE TUNE

DAME. Hi, love your red hat, where'ya from?

BARONESS. Texas! Yours is darling. Where you from?

DAME. New Jersey.

BARONESS. Wanna play?

DAME. Sure.

BARONESS & DAME.

WELL I'M NOT GONNA SIT IN A ROCKIN' CHAIR
AND A WONDER WHERE LIFE WENT.
WHY 70 IS NOT TOO LATE
TO BE ELECTED PRESIDENT.
OH AMELIA, WHEN I GROW UP
YOU'VE INSPIRED ME TO FLY.
NOW THAT I'M FINALLY MAKING TIME

(They harmonize. Other women enter with band instruments.)

ALL.

FOR ME, MYSELF AND I.

BARONESS.

WELL MY STATUS AS A SEX SYMBOL
MIGHT BE SOMEWHAT PRECARIOUS.
BUT I BELIEVE THAT I POSSESS
NOTHING SHORT OF A STRADIVARIUS.
WELL MY REPERTOIRE IS SO MUCH BROADER
THAN IT WAS WHEN I WAS YOUNG.

ALL.

AND MY ENCORE IS DARN SURE
GONNA BE IN THE KEY OF FUN.

(Dance break.)

LADY. *(pointing toward* **MARYANNE** *sitting on the side to join the group)* MaryAnne!

ALL.

'CAUSE THE OLDER THE FIDDLE
THE SWEETER THE TUNE.
THERE'S NO SHORTCUT TO PERFECTION.
IT JUST TAKES MANY A MOON.

AND I PREFER SEPTEMBER SONG

TO THE ONE I PLAYED IN JUNE.
'CAUSE THE OLDER THE FIDDLE

THE SWEETER THE TUNE.
OH YES THE OLDER THE FIDDLE
THE SWEETER THE TUNE.

CONTESSA. *(huffing and puffing)* Come on MaryAnne. You need a margarita. *(All, except **LADY**, leave laughing.)*

PLAYOFF MUSIC

*(The girls and **MARYANNE** exit as **LADY** steps forward.)*

LADY LABRADOR NOIR

LADY. *(fanning herself with her hat)* Well, that was fun! *(Noticing that hat in her hand, she speaks to the audience:)* Isn't it lovely. My 8-year-old granddaughter Rachel gave me it to me. Five years ago I was visiting my daughter, Maryanne, back in Michigan – I couldn't take those winters any more – and my heaven's, how my granddaughter loved to play dress up! We would have very elaborate tea parties with her stuffed Black Lab named Chester. After I came back home I got a very lovely package in the mail. Inside was this sweet floppy hat and an even sweeter note that said –

"Dear Nana – I miss you. I like having you here. I got you this pretty hat so you can play dress up at home. I love you."

Well, that sure made me think...

SONG: CELEBRATE
Lyrics by Gretchen Cryer, Music by Stephen Lawrence

CELEBRATE THE CHILDREN
BLESS 'EM EVERY ONE
CELEBRATE THE GOOD TIMES
DRESSIN' UP AND HAVIN' LOTS OF FUN.
PUTTIN' ON MY RED HAT
SET MY SPIRIT FREE
CELEBRATE THE CHILDREN
CELEBRATE WITH ME

I am a widow. It seems funny, but I was married longer than I was anything else. And then all of a sudden I wasn't. Tom was just gone.

You know how in the movies there's a tastefully shot scene where the couple have a tender parting as violins hum a plaintive tune, their hands are joined and then one hand slips away? That sure wasn't me. One minute Tom was on the couch watching Emeril on the Food Channel while I put the kettle on, and by the time I brought out two cups of Earl Grey and some Mint Milanos, he was just gone. How do you say good-bye to someone who's already left?

CELEBRATE THE MEM'RIES
BLESS 'EM EVERY ONE
CELEBRATE THE GOOD TIMES
SURE, WE HAD OUR FIGHTS, THEN THEY WERE DONE
CELEBRATE A LIFETIME
GOOD AS IT COULD BE
CELEBATE THE MEMORIES
CELEBRATE WITH ME.

So I did the widow thing, took the calls, wrote the notes, got on with getting on.

But between you and me, I was just going through the motions. Then adding insult to injury I had one of those birthdays with a *zero* – a big one. Well I don't mind telling you, it was a bit of a turd in the swimming pool. Anyway, I read a feature in the paper about a group of "women of a certain age." They're widows who call themselves The Royal House of Stuart, Florida.

So I decided to check it out. I wore my granddaughter's sweet floppy hat and went to a lovely brunch. We talked and laughed about the silliest things; I'd forgotten how important that is. As my granddaughter says, "It makes my heart smile." That's pretty hard to beat.

So, in honor of my granddaughter and her stuffed Black Lab Chester, I am now Lady Labrador Noir!

CELEBRATE THE SISTERS
BLESS 'EM EVERY ONE
CELEBRATE THE GOOD TIMES
DRESSIN' UP AND HAVIN' LOTS OF FUN.

CELEBRATE THE FRIENDSHIP
LET YOUR SPIRIT FREE.
CELEBRATE THE SISTERS,
CELEBRATE WITH ME

CELEBRATE A NEW DAY
CELEBRATE THE DAWN
CELEBRATE THE SUNRISE
PICKIN' UP AND FINALLY MOVIN' ON.
IF YOU FEEL LIKE DANCING
LET YOUR SPIRIT FREE
PUTTIN' ON MY RED HAT
UNDERNEATH THE BLUE SKIES
EVERY DAY'S A NEW LIFE –

CELEBRATE WITH ME
CELEBRATE WITH ME
CELEBRATE, WITH ME!

*(**MARYANNE** enters wearing a cowboy hat with **BARONESS**. Breaks applause.)*

MARYANNE. Yee Haw!

LADY. Where have you been?

MARYANNE. I was just hanging out with that Baroness. Boy she really has it all together. She doesn't need a man to make her feel complete. I envy that!

BARONESS. Looks can be deceiving, my dear. Two weeks ago *(We hear a phone ring.)* I got a call *(ringing again)* from my friend *(ringing again)*...

(Lighting shift. Two weeks prior.)

(answering her Blackberry) Oh, hi, Anita. – You what? – What guy? – Now, hold on a minute – I said I "wanted" to date again. I didn't say I was ready. – I am NOT a chicken. – All right, WHEN? *(She refers to her calendar.)* Uh...Saturday's no good. – Monday night...no good. – Thursday? Anita, how 'bout never...does that work for ya? Look, girlfriend, the thing is, I just don't have anything to wear on a date anymore. – What! Anita, you are like a dog with a bone! – Yeah, yeah, bye. *(She hangs up and exits.)*

DAME'S EMPTY NEST

DAME. *(enters carrying shopping bags, singing)*
LA DA DEE DA DA DA DEE DA DEE DA.

Ever since I was a little girl I have loved Hollywood musicals. My favorites are the ones with Audrey Hepburn – because to me she *was* style. I have always wanted one of those fabulous hats like she wore in *My Fair Lady.* Anyway, last week I saw one on EBAY. An exact replica. So I bid on it and I won! I almost died. It was so beautiful! But I would never have the nerve to wear something like that.

Oh, I'm no star. No way. I never wanted to be in the school play. I was content just sewing costumes. Backstage. Out of the spotlight. That's sorta what I love about being wife and mom; working backstage; helping the ones onstage to shine. And honestly, after seeing them through term papers, soccer games, chipped teeth, throwing up, driving lessons, fender benders, one broken leg and one ER appendectomy – I still think it's the best job in the world – I am Home Tech Support 24/7 I am always there for them.

Or was. One is a senior in college, one's in law school at Harvard and my youngest just became a tattoo artist in Las Vegas. My husband is an obstetrician and you know what *that* means – he's always on call. *(She takes a deep breath.)*

But…I have no complaints. No complaints whatsoever.

SONG: MY EMPTY NEST
Music & Lyrics by Carol Hall.

(at first gentle and contemplative)

DAME.

ALL AT ONCE
JUST LIKE THAT
HOUSE SO PERFECT
HOUSE SO CLEAN

HERE I SIT
IN MY CHAIR
GUESS I'LL READ A MAGAZINE
MAYBE MAKE MYSELF A CUP OF TEA
THE KIDS ARE GROWN
AND NOW MY SCHEDULE'S FREE

ISN'T IT QUIET?
ISN'T IT PEACEFUL?
FLUFFIN' UP PILLOWS
IN MY EMPTY NEST

NO ONE HAS THE MEASLES
NO ONE NEEDS A SHIRT
NO ONE GOT DETENTION
NO ONE TRACKED IN DIRT
NO ONE LOST THE GERBIL
NO ONE LOST THE GAME
THE KIDS ARE GROWN
AND NOTHING IS THE SAME

ALL AT ONCE
JUST LIKE THAT
TIME TO SPEND AND
TIME TO BE
TAKE A TRIP
TAKE A NAP
THINK OF SOMETHING JUST FOR ME…
MAYBE LEARN THE TANGO
DO FUNG SHUI
'CAUSE NO ONE CALLED TO ASK
IF I'D MAKE COSTUMES FOR THE PLAY

ISN'T IT QUIET?
SOMEBODY MAKE SOME NOISE
PEACEFUL?
IT'S TIME FOR OPRAH

(fluffin' up pillows)

COME GET ME OUTTA THIS
EMPTY NEST

I SHOULD SEE THE WORLD NOW
TAKE IN ALL THE SIGHTS
KATMANDU OR PARIS
SPARKLING DAYS AND NIGHTS
GUESS I NEED ADVENTURES
YES I NEED SOME FUN
SOMETIMES THOUGH, I NEED SOMEONE
WHO NEEDS THEIR LAUNDRY DONE!

ISN'T IT *(offstage voices)* QUIET...
I MIGHT LEARN ORAGAMI
(offstage voices) PEACEFUL...
OR CHANTING WITH A SWAMI...
OHM, OHM, OHM!
NOBODY NEEDS A "MOMMY"
IN MY EMPTY NEST.

SUDDENLY THE HOUSE FEELS QUITE BIZARRE
THERE'S NOTHING IN THE GARAGE EXCEPT A CAR
NOT A TWINKIE, NOT A DING-DONG DO I SEE
AND EVERY TIME THE PHONE RINGS...
IT'S FOR ME.

(spoken) "TELEMARKETERS!!!"

(Now she's in a tizzy.)

NO ONE HAS THE MEASLES
HOUSE SO PERFECT
HOUSE SO CLEAN
NO ONE GOT DETENTION
GUESS I'LL READ A MAGAZINE
NO ONE LOST THE GERBIL
NO ONE LOST THE GAME
THE KIDS ARE GROWN
THE KIDS ARE GROWN
THE KIDS ARE GROWN
I'M GOING CRAZY!

(A music break...a revelation. "On the other hand.")

SOME CRAZY PART OF ME
SEES OPPORTUNITY
THESE YEARS AHEAD MIGHT BE THE BEST

SO WHO NEEDS THE PILLOWS?

I DON'T WANT THE PILLOWS

GET RID OF THE PILLOWS!

I'M GETTING OUTTA

THIS EMPTY NEST!!!

(The big Hollywood musical ending takes **DAME** *out the door.)*

BARONESS CROSSOVER

(Continuing her flashback. **BARONESS** *appears on a sidewalk carrying shopping bags. She pauses to look at a dress she just bought, and then continues on to the next store.)*

JUST LIKE ME

*(***PRINCESS** *enters carrying a shoulder bag and satchel. She puts down her stuff and looks in her purse.)*

PRINCESS. Keys…keys. I always put them back in the little zipper pocket.

(She looks – no keys.)

WHEN I WAS LITTLE, I'D ALWAYS LOST THINGS
MITTENS, LUNCHBOX, HATS AND HOMEWORK
I STILL REMEMBER MY FATHER TOLD ME,
"GOOD THING THAT YOUR HEAD'S SCREWED ON.

(spoken) Oh, my other bag…

AND THEN IN COLLEGE I STILL WOULD LOSE THINGS
KEYS OR LIPSTICK, PURSE OR EARRINGS
MY BOYFRIEND GAVE ME HIS LETTER SEATER
THREE DAYS LATER, IT WAS GONE

JUST LIKE ME
IT WAS A GIVEN THAT LOSING THINGS WAS
JUST LIKE ME
THEY ALWAYS THOUGHT IT WAS SO AMUSING
BUT WHO'D HAVE FIGURED I'D END UP LOSING…

(spoken) Oh I remember now, I dropped them in my make-up bag with my change.

THEN I GOT MARRIED, IT SEEMED SO SIMPLE
TWENTY YEARS OF JOY AND MAGIC
WHERE OTHER COUPLES WERE COURTING DANGER
HAPPINESS WAS ALL WE FOUND

IT WAS SO EASY TO TAKE FOR GRANTED
SOMEWHERE WE BEGAN TO LOSE IT
UNTIL ONE DAY YOU WERE JUST A STRANGER
WISHING I WAS NOT AROUND.

JUST LIKE ME
I'D CHANGE MY HAIR AND WARDROBE SO HE'D
JUST LIKE ME
MY LIFE WAS SUDDENLY SO CONFUSING
I'D NEVER DREAMED I COULD END UP LOSING YOU.

TO FEEL YOU JUST SLIP AWAY
WITHOUT QUITE KNOWING WHY
THE WAY WE'D BOTH DENY THAT ANYTHING WAS
WRONG
SENSING A LOSS I COULDN'T PUT MY FINGER ON

NOT KNOWING WHAT TO DO
EXCEPT TO THINK IT'S TRUE
ONCE I HAVE IT THEN IT'S GONE.

NOW THAT I'M OLDER I STILL FORGET THINGS
GLASSES, NUMBERS, NAMES, PRESCRIPTIONS
BUT I REMEMBER THE DAY YOU TOLD ME
THE OTHER WOMAN WAS THRITY-FIVE

AND I REMEMBER THE LAME EXCUSES
SOMETHING DIFFERENT
NEW ADVENTURE
HOW SHE REMINDED YOU OF THE OLD ME
WELL, BUDDY, LISTEN I'M STILL ALIVE!
JUST LIKE ME
YOU FOUND SOMEONE TO REPLACE ME WHO WAS
JUST LIKE ME

YOU WERE SUPPOSED TO BE DONE WITH CHOOSING
WELL NOW I'M FINALLY DONE WITH LOSING –

WITHOUT YOU HERE I AM FINDING HOW TO
JUST LIKE ME
AND NOW THE ANSWERS ARE LESS CONFUSING
AND HOW IRONIC AND HOW AMUSING
I FIND MYSELF AS I END UP LOSING –

(She finds her keys in her pocket.) – YOU!

(With a triumphant little laugh, she exits.)

(Back at the party. **MARYANNE** *and* **LADY** *enter.* **LADY** *is snacking on a large chocolate bar.)*

LADY. Mmmmm…

MARYANNE. Mother –

LADY. What? It's soooo good. And I'm so hungry. I thought I would have downed five or six slices of cake by this point in the evening.

MARYANNE. Well, I'm sorry my existential crisis is conflicting with your feeding schedule.

LADY. I don't appreciate your tone. We're at the age where food has taken the place of sex. In fact, I've just had a mirror put over my kitchen table.

MARYANNE. Mother! That's gross!

LADY. Honey, you think you're the only one with a libido? Why just this week I found a place where I could meet a sexy, young, studlette who is attracted to a woman of my age...at Borders...under FICTION!

DAME. *(entering)* My doctor, he said I had to take this medication for the REST of my life...it says here NO REFILLS!

BARONESS. *(entering)*

YOU KNOW YOU'RE GETTING OLD WHEN YOU'RE
SITTING IN THE ROCKER...AND CAN'T GET IT
STARTED!

DAME. Note to children:

Last Will and Testament:

Being of sound mind...I spent ALL my money! AND yours!

CONTESSA. *(entering)* These days, I try to use my time wisely…If I have to I bend over, I try to think if there is anything else I need to do while I'm down there!

LADY. *(exiting)* But don't worry, MaryAnne, you will never grow older if you carry your inner child with you.

MARYANNE. Inner Child? With the hot flashes I've been having lately, I'd burn the poor little thing at THE STAKE!

DUCHESS. *(entering)* Well I don't have hot flashes, Honey – I have "power surges!"

SONG: MY OVEN'S STILL HOT!
Lyrics by Anthony Dodge & Marcia Milgrom Dodge,
Music by Beth Falcone

DUCHESS/CONTESSA/BARONESS/LADY/DAME.

THERE MAY BE SNOW

SNOW-HO-HO-HO

ON MY ROOFTOP

DA-DA-DA-DOP

MY FOUNDATION

NA-NA-NA-NA

SLIGHTLY SHOT

SHA DA DA DA DA SHOT

BUT IF YOU COME

CUH-HUH-HUH-HUM

IN MY KITCHEN DARLIN'

CUH-HUH-HUH-HUM

YOO-HOO WILL FIND

DA-DA-DA

MY OVEN'S STILL HOT!
YEAH! OOH

SO VERY HOT!
MY LOVIN' OVEN, MY OVEN
MY OVEN'S STILL HOT!

BABY
COME-UH-COME-UH
COME-UH-COME COME

MY LOVIN' OVEN,
MY OVEN'S STILL HOT!

MY AGING WALLS

WA-HA-HA-HALLS

MAY BE BOWED

DOH-DOH-DOH-DOH

WANTING SERVICE

GIVE IT TO ME

IN MORE THAN ONE
SPOT

HERE, HERE, AND HERE!

BUT IF YOU COME

CUH-HUH-HUH-HUM
IN MY KITCHEN DARLIN'   CUH-HUH-HUH-HUM
YOU WILL FIND

DA-DA-DA

MY OVENS STILL
HOT! YEAH!   MY OVEN'S STILL,
YEAH, YEAH YEAH YEAH   MY LOVIN OVEN, MY
YEAH   OVEN,
BABY   MY OVEN'S STILL
COME-UH-COME-UH-   HOT! MY LOVIN' OVEN,
COME-UH
COME UH ON   MY OVEN'S STILL HOT!
YEAH!

COME HERE SWEETNESS   OOH WAH OOH WAH
                               OOH

LET MOMMA GIVE YOU
A THRILL
I GUARANTEE YOU
WON'T NEED
THAT LITTLE BLUE
PILL!

                               IT'S NOT THAT COLD
                               YOU SHOULD BE TOLD
                               COME ON!

COME ON

                               BE BOLD!

BE BOLD

                               I'M NOT THAT OLD!
(spoken) Sing it Girls!

                               I'M NOT THAT OLD!

(sung in a high falsetto voice:)
THERE MAY BE SNOW

                               SNOW-HO-HO-HO

ON MY ROOFTOP

                DA-DA-DA DOP

MAYBE SOME WRINKLES

                ZA-DA-DA-DOT!

OKAY A LOT.

                A LOT!

THERE'S A LOT.
BUT IF YOU COME

                COME

IN MY KITCHEN
DARLIN'   COME
YOO-HOO WILL FIND

                DA-DA-DA

MY OVEN'S STILL HOT! MY OVEN'S STILL HOT!
YEAH!   YEAH!

OOH BABY,   MY LOVIN' OVEN, MY
                OVEN,
COME-UH-COME-UH   MY OVEN'S STILL HOT!
COME-UH-COME COME MY LOVIN' OVEN, MY
                OVEN
DARLIN'   MY OVEN'S STILL – HOT!

I'M ON FIRE!

(They exit.)

PRINCESS. *(entering singing)* I'M ON FIRE!!! Nothin' says lovin' like something from the oven! That Duchess is pretty amazing, isn't she?

MARYANNE. She's like the poster child for hormone replacement therapy.

PRINCESS. Look honey, this ought to prove that fifty is just a number–a lovely number! Look at it this way, you gently *turn* fifty, then it gets a little tougher as you *reach* sixty, then by God, you *hit* seventy and for the next ten years, if you're lucky, you're *pushin'* eighty…and not daisies!

MARYANNE. You don't understand. For me, it's a big fat marker that was supposed to reveal how I measured up to my dreams. You know, I graduated from college on my way to becoming a great writer. Oh yeah, I was going to make my mark in the world, but Mom said: "You need something to fall back on." So, when I got married, I started teaching. It was "temporary." I taught school all day and wrote all night.

PRINCESS. And?

MARYANNE. And, I was so busy trying to hang on to that dream that I put off having a baby 'til it was almost too late. Thank God we didn't miss out on Rachel!

PRINCESS. See?!

MARYANNE. But I was supposed to "have it all."

PRINCESS. You have a great career!

MARYANNE. I'm still teaching third grade, and I love it. And now I fall asleep grading papers.

PRINCESS. It's a phase, but little Rachel is a great joy.

MARYANNE. Little Rachel, who used to need my help to get the part straight on her ponytails, is on the verge of running off with a kid on a motorcycle and getting a tattoo!

PRINCESS. Hey, teenagers have dreams too! She's wanting to find out how GOOD it is and you are trying to REMEMBER!

MARYANNE. *(not laughing, not listening, continuing)* Frankly, she reminds me of the me I USED to be, wide open, running it right up to the edge. But somewhere along the way, I opted to play it safe, slow it down, and here is where it got me…scared to go the mailbox, cause I know my AARP CARD IS COMING!

PRINCESS. Don't be such a "Debbie-Downer!" Fifty is finding a new dream.

MARYANNE. Fifty is forced retirement. Terrifies me. What would I do? I don't even have the courage anymore to try something new.

(PRINCESS gasps.)

I can't!

PRINCESS. "Can't" is a nasty four-letter word.

(**PRINCESS** *exits.*)

MARYANNE. And I thought it was just a contraction.

(*MARYANNE follows her.*)

LADY & DAME STORIES
(*Two women are knitting. They are the best of friends and know each other so well that they can finish each other's sentences. Or in this case, sweetly correct the other.*)

LADY. We saw a program last week on PBS –

DAME. – It was on OPRAH –

LADY. – It was on OPRAH. And there was a woman on who was a Business Psychiatrist –

DAME. – Business Psychologist –

LADY. – She was a Business Psychologist, and she was talking about…now how did she put it – ?

DAME. – Corporations use a paradigm for organizational information transfer –

LADY. Oh sure. An exemplar to facilitate research mobilization through an observational model called –

LADY & DAME. Peer Mentoring!

LADY. And then you said –

DAME. – It was you –

LADY. – And then I said, "That's just like our group!" That's what we do, we reach out and connect and we give each other confidantes –

DAME. – Confidence –

LADY. – We give each other confidence.

DAME. Although I am also your confidante.

LADY. Thanks! Anyway, we have this friend, Barbara. She's a super gal. Her husband is one of those Oncologists –

DAME. – He's an Ophthalmologist.

LADY. He's an Ophthalmologist. Her one complaint is that now that the kids are out of the house, she has a lot of free time on her hands and her hubby is a golf nut, a real snacker.

DAME. Hacker.

LADY. Whatever. Anyway, she decided to try to learn golf so she could share some time with her man. So she rented some clubs and took a GOLF lesson with a pro. Well, it was the worst day of her life! She said she felt like a ginseng knife –

DAME. – Ginsu knife –

LADY. – Like a ginsu knife – she sliced, she diced, she hooked, she sank –

DAME. – She shanked.

LADY. She SHANKED it in the water, honey – and it SANK!

DAME. FORE!

LADY. SPLASH! *(They laugh.)* Well, she was SO embarrassed she QUIT!

DAME. But when she told that story at our Friday Tea, one of our friends offered to give her some pointers.

(**PRINCESS** *enters as* **GOLF PRO**. **DUCHESS** *enters as* **GOLF DUFFER**. *We see the re-enactment.)*

SONG: YES WE CAN
Lyrics by Kathie Lee Gifford, Music by David Friedman

GOLF PRO (PRINCESS).
FIRST OF ALL, YOU MUST RELAX,
BREATHE DEEP, NOW YOU'RE READY TO START.
GRIP THE CLUB LIKE THIS
FEET SHOULDER WIDTH APART.
TRY NOT TO MOVE YOUR HEAD.
KEEP YOUR EYES ON THE BACK OF THE BALL.
TURN YOUR BODY AS YOU TAKE A SWING
THERE'S REALLY NOTHING TO IT AT ALL.

GOLF DUFFER (DUCHESS). I can't!

GOLF PRO (PRINCESS). Yes, you can!
IF YOU SETTLE FOR WHAT YOU'VE GOT,
YOU DESERVE WHAT YOU GET.
YOU CAN'T GO SWIMMING
IF YOU'RE NOT WILLING TO GET WET.
YOU CAN'T TASTE THE OYSTER
IF YOU'RE SCARED TO SWALLOW THE PEARL.

YOU CAN'T BECOME THE WOMAN YOU WANT
IF YOU'RE TOO COMFORTABLE WITH THE GIRL.

(PRO gives DUFFER her red golf visor.)

LADY & DAME.
SHE LOOKED RIGHT AT THAT GOLF BALL,
GRIPPED THE CLUB JUST RIGHT.
TURNED HER BODY, FOLLOWED THROUGH,
AND WATCHED IT FLY, RIGHT OUT OF SIGHT.

GOLF DUFFER (DUCHESS). I did it!!!!!

GOLF PRO (PRINCESS). You're a natural!

(GOLF PRO and DUFFER exit together. The two women applaud them.)

LADY. Or, take our friend Theresa. Her doctor told her she should start going to someone named Jim.

DAME. – Start going to The Gym.

LADY. – She should start going to the gym. And she said:

(CONTESSA enters as YOGA GAL.)

CONTESSA. "Exercise? I'm in no shape to exercise!"

DAME. The only exercise she gets is pushing her luck.

LADY. Then someone suggested she give Yogurt a try –

DAME. – Suggested she try Yoga. So she immediately went out and –

LADY & DAME. – Got a brochure.

YOGA GAL (CONTESSA).
DON'T YOU JUST ADORE BROCHURES?
SO FULL OF INFORMATION!
YOU CAN DO SO MUCH
WITHOUT PARTICIPATION.
YOU CAN GET A WORKOUT
SIMPLY TURNING A PAGE OR TWO.
DOWNWARD DOG
CAMEL,
TREE POSE
COW.
WHO KNEW YOGA WAS SO EASY TO DO?

*(***PRINCESS** *enters as* **YOGA GURU** *with a purple yoga mat. She demonstrates yoga as she sings.)*

YOGA GURU (PRINCESS).

IF YOU SETTLE FOR WHAT YOU'VE GOT,
YOU DESERVE WHAT YOU GET.
LIFE'S A TIGHT-ROPE,
BUT YOUR FRIENDS ARE YOUR SAFETY NET.
TO STRETCH BEYOND YOUR LIMITS,
SIMPLY BEND FROM HEAD TO TOE.

THERE ISN'T ANYTHING YOU CAN'T DO,
GET READY,
GET SET, GIRL – GO!

(She lays down the purple mat.)

LADY & DAME.

SO SHE STEPPED OUT ON THAT MAT,
AND SHE REACHED UP TO THE SKY,
BENT AND TOUCHED THE TIPS OF HER TOES.
LOOK WHAT HAPPENS WHEN YOU TRY!

YOGA GAL (CONTESSA). I did it!

*(***PRINCESS** *and* **CONTESSA** *exit.)*

LADY. We *also* have a friend. Let's just call her MaryAnne.

DAME. – Because that's her real name –

LADY. – Who always wanted to learn to tap dance. Oh she meant to, but Life kept getting in the way, as *impractical* gave way to *sensible.*

DAME. Which makes no sense, because there is no expiration date on FUN.

LADY. So one of our friends took her to a tap lesson where she decided she'd take the step and change her balls.

DAME. Step-ball-change.

*(***BARONESS** *as* **TAP WANNABE** *and* **MARYANNE** *enter adlibbing:* **BARONESS***: "Come on, it'll be fun."* **MARY-ANNE***: "I don't know.")*

TAP WANNABE (BARONESS).

I KNOW WHAT YOU'RE THINKING HERE.
GOT NO RHYTHM, GOT TWO LEFT FEET.

MARYANNE. *(spoken)* Exactly!
　　I CAN BARELY WALK
　　HOW CAN I KEEP UP WITH THE BEAT?

TAP WANNABE (BARONESS).
　　I'M EMBARRASSED WHEN I MOVE MY BUTT
　　IT KEEPS MOVING EVEN WHEN I STOP

MARYANNE.
　　I'M AFRAID I'LL TRIP.

TAP WANNABE (BARONESS).
　　AND I'M AFRAID MY UTERUS WILL DROP.

　　(spoken) Oh, here she is.

　　(PRINCESS *enters as* **TAP TEACHER** *with purple tap shoes.)*

TAP TEACHER (PRINCESS). *(spoken)* Ladies.
　　IF YOU SETTLE FOR WHAT YOU'VE GOT,
　　YOU DESERVE WHAT YOU GET
　　IT'S OK TO DO "THE TIME-STEP" BUT NOT "THE FRET".
　　YOU CAN DO "THE STEP-BALL-CHANGE",
　　BUT STOP DOIN' "THE DOUBT",
　　WE PROMISE IF YOU'LL ONLY TRY
　　YOU'LL TAP YOUR CELLULITE OUT!

MARYANNE. I did it!

GOLF DUFFER (DUCHESS).
　　I CAN DRIVE THE FAIRWAY – FORE!

ALL WOMEN.
　　YES SHE CAN, CAN!

YOGA GAL (CONTESSA).
　　I CAN DO THE "DOWN DOG"

ALL WOMEN.
　　YES SHE CAN, CAN!

TAP WANNABE (BARONESS).
　　SHE CAN TAP HER BRAINS OUT!

ALL WOMEN.
　　YES SHE/I CAN, CAN, CAN!

　　CAN, CAN

IF WE TRY WE CAN, CAN,
IF WE TRY WE CAN CAN,

IF WE TRY WE/CAN
IF WE TRY WE/CAN

(Pull back for big kick line.)

IF – WE –

SETTLE FOR WHAT WE'VE GOT,
WE DESERVE WHAT WE GET.

THERE'S TOO MUCH LIVIN' THAT'S LEFT TO DO
TO GIVE UP YET.

YOU'RE LOOKIN' AT WOMEN
WHO HAVE ONLY JUST BEGUN

TO OVERCOME THEIR FEARS,
TO REV UP ALL THEIR GEARS
AND ROAR DOWN THAT STREET OF "SOMEDAY"
DREAMS
UNTIL WE MAKE THEM COME TRUE.

TOGETHER WE
TOGETHER WE
TOGETHER WE CAN DO IT

ME – AND –
YOU!

PLAYOFF MUSIC

CAN, CAN IF WE TRY WE CAN, CAN,
IF WE TRY WE CAN CAN,
IF WE TRY WE CAN!

SHOPPING

(In **BARONESS**'s *flashback. Underscore of "Older the Fiddle."* **BARONESS** *enters from one of the upstage doors, now a dressing room in a boutique. She is trying on clothes. She looks in the mirror and is not happy.)*

BARONESS. Remember my buddy, Anita? Well, she fixed me up with this guy in her firm. I was looking for a guy like George Clooney. A naked George Clooney. A blind, naked George Clooney. But anyway…first date in two years and I feel like a damn teenager! I tried on my pre-divorce cocktail dress and felt like a middle-aged harlot. Then I put on my expensive and stunningly simple business suit and felt like an old-fashioned ball-buster! So Anita said, "Go get something NEW, girlfriend. Something hip and with it." So here I am in Limbo. LIMBO – that's the name of the store.

(**DUCHESS** *enters from another one of the upstage dressing room doors.*)

(*She is dressed in sexy lingerie.*)

BARONESS. Well, look at you!

DUCHESS. Girl, please! I'm just tryin' to keep my oven hot. Well, look at you. You've tried on that same outfit three times.

BARONESS. I know. I'm just having cold feet about this date.

DUCHESS. You better live up to that cowboy hat, Miss Thing!

BARONESS. I hate shopping.

DUCHESS. Honey, take it from me, shopping is better than sex.

BARONESS. Really?

DUCHESS. Yeah, if you're not satisfied after shopping you can always exchange it for something better.

(*She exits as* **DAME** *enters with shopping bags humming to herself.*)

DAME. Well, look at you....

BARONESS. Hell, I've been here two hours and I can't find anything I like!

DAME. Oh, I just take stuff home and copy the patterns. Take home-copy-return.

BARONESS. Well, I can't sew.

DAME. Well I can! I spent my whole life making costumes for other people. (*She whips out a tape measure.*) What do you need?

BARONESS. I don't know – I'm going on a date.

DAME. Great!

*(As **DAME** takes each of her measurements…)*

BARONESS. Something not too tight. Something not too short. Not too low!

DAME. What do you want, a mu-mu?

BARONESS. Hell, I don't remember how to be on a date anymore!

SEE MY STATUS AS A SEX SYMBOL
MIGHT BE SOMEWHAT PRECARIOUS

DAME.

BUT I BELIEVE THAT YOU POSSESS
NOTHING SHORT OF A STRADIVARIOUS
OH THE LATEST RIFF MAY TURN THEIR HEADS
BUT EXPERIENCE MAKES THEM SWOON
'CAUSE THE OLDER THE FIDDLE – Remember!
THE SWEETER THE TUNE!

*(She pulls **BARONESS** off the stage as **CONTESSA**, **LADY** and **DUCHESS** enter with shopping bags.)*

LADY, DUCHESS.

OLDER ISN'T SUCH A DRAG CONTRARY TO
CONVENTION
IT'S TAKEN ME A LIFETIME TO UNDERSTAND
HARMONIC TENSION
IN ALL THOSE HUSTLE BUSTLE YEARS
LIFE WAS TOO STACCATO
BUT NOW I PLAY WITH EASE AND GRACE
WITH A SIMPLE DOWN HOME LEGATO.

*(As they hold the note, **DAME** and **BARONESS** re-enter. **BARONESS** is wearing a great, sexy dress.)*

DAME. Girls!

LADY & DUCHESS. Well, look at you!

*(They fluff **BARONESS** as she preens in the mirror, hand her a little sequined bag.)*

LADY, DUCHESS, DAME.
>WHEN YOU'RE A FRESH FACED PRODIGY
>YOUR PLAYIN' MAY BE NIFTY
>BUT YOU DON'T REALLY KNOW THE SCORE
>UNTIL YOU'RE OVER FIFTY.

BARONESS.
>AND IF I JUST REPEAT AND FADE, I'D BE…

ALL.
>HANGIN' UP MY BOW TOO SOON!
>CAUSE THE OLDER THE FIDDLE, THE SWEETER THE
>TUNE
>OH YES, THE OLDER THE FIDDLE, THE SWEETER THE
>TUNE!

LADY. Hey, can you make me one of those?

*(They wave goodbye as **BARONESS** exits to go on her date. They exit as the attic set tracks on.)*

PRINCESS MONOLOG
*(The slanted roof of an attic. A gabled window sneaks light through its slats. Everywhere you can see is stuff: boxes, bags, luggage and memories – some kept, some forgotten. **PRINCESS** is busily going through and cleaning out what turns out to be her parents' attic.)*

PRINCESS. I found this simple little hat when I lost my mom. We were great friends, I'm happy to say. Mom loved life…travel, parties, telling an off-color story. She often said, "Polly, don't take life too seriously or you'll never get out of it alive." Mom also said that the price she paid for being fabulous was her unfortunate affair with Gene…Breast Cancer Gene. He was an ardent suitor and Mom a born fighter.

After Mom was gone – it's still hard to say those words – I promised to help Dad clear out their attic. Mom was allergic to recycling, and consequently kept a wonderful collection of "Life Debris." I spent hours pouring over photographs and gathering a virtual time capsule of clothes.

And then I found it. On a shelf sandwiched between my accordion file of report cards and a box of Super-8 movie reels was this hatbox. A little ray of sunlight shone right on it, from the slatted window on the gable. A heavenly light.

Have you ever had one of those moments when you feel something was going to happen? Something special? This was one of those moments. I took the hatbox in my hands and sat down on my old camp Sea Gull footlocker.

Mom had already been on my mind all day, but when I opened that box I could see her right there *beside* me. *(She takes a hat out of a hat box.)* She must have worn it sometime after World War II, back when everyone wore hats. It was obviously a special hat because it still looked new.

The minute I saw it I knew I'd wear my Mom's hat – her legacy to me to always stay a fighter. The only thing I've changed is to add this pink satin ribbon.

I wear this hat to remind me that I am also a fighter. The pink ribbon is for Mom.

(UNDERSCORE)

When I found myself alone last year, I thought, "What would Mom have me do now?" Something brave I'm sure. So I put an ad in a singles service online: "mature woman seeks evolved male." I got some good responses but always the inevitable question: "How old are you?" When I told the truth, the emails stopped.

Oh, I'm not giving up. I have faith. But you know, it's does take a lot of courage to be single at this point in my life. When I go out, I see couples everywhere. Sometimes I feel that they just look right through me.

SONG: INVISIBLE
Music & Lyrics by Melissa Manchester and Sharon
Vaughn

PRINCESS.

CAN YOU SEE ME?
TELL ME YOU CAN SEE ME.
WHEN DID I VANISH INTO THIN AIR?
I DON'T REMEMBER
WHEN I BECAME AN EMBER
AND NOT A FLARE.

WHERE DOES THE FIRE GO
THAT BURNS BUT DOESN'T SHOW?
I DON'T KNOW.

PRINCESS & DUCHESS.

I DON'T KNOW.

DUCHESS.

WHERE'S MY SHADOW?
I USED TO CAST A SHADOW.
DID THEY TURN OUT THE MIDDAY SUN?
IT'S CRAZY HOW THEY IGNORE
AND MAKE ME INTO NO ONE
MUST I JUST DISAPPEAR,
WHILE I'M STILL STANDING HERE?

PRINCESS & DUCHESS.

INVISIBLE
AS A GHOST I FLOAT ON BY.
INVISIBLE
AS A MOONLESS EMPTY SKY.
BUT THE OPEN EYES OF A LOVING HEART
CAN LIFT THE VEIL AND, WHEN THE CURTAINS PART,

DUCHESS.

THERE I'LL BE
I WON'T BE

PRINCESS & DUCHESS.

INVISIBLE

MARYANNE. *(entering)* See, that's what I'm afraid of. I'm afraid I won't be MaryAnne anymore.

WHEN I TOUCH YOU,
DOES IT REALLY TOUCH YOU?
IS IT THE MEMORY OF ME YOU LOVE?

MARYANNE & DUCHESS.

HAVE WE FADED?
GROWN COMFORTABLE AND JADED?

ALL.

IS THAT ENOUGH

MARYANNE.

WHO KNOWS WHERE FEELINGS GO –
THAT STILL BURN
BUT JUST BURN SLOW.

ALL THREE.

INVISIBLE
AS A GHOST I FLOAT ON BY
INVISIBLE AS A MOONLESS EMPTY SKY.
BUT THE OPEN EYES OF A LOVING HEART
CAN LIFT THE VEIL AND WHEN THE CURTAINS PART

PRINCESS.

THERE I'LL BE

DUCHESS.

I WON'T BE

PRINCESS.

INVISIBLE

DUCHESS & MARYANNE.

INVISIBLE

PRINCESS/DUCHESS/MARYANNE.

NO, I WON'T GO AWAY.

DUCHESS.

I'M NOT INVISIBLE

PRINCESS & MARYANNE.

INVISIBLE

ALL THREE.

I HAVE A LOT TO SAY
ABOUT WHERE I'M GOING AND WHERE I'VE BEEN.
WHEN YOU NEED THE COMFORT OF A DEAR OLD
FRIEND,

PRINCESS.

> THERE I'LL BE

DUCHESS.

> THERE I'LL BE

PRINCESS.

> THERE I'LL BE

DUCHESS.

> THERE I'LL BE

DUCHESS/PRINCESS/MARYANNE.

> THERE I'LL BE

DAME.

> THERE I'LL BE!

CONTESSA.

> THERE I'LL BE

BARONESS.

> THERE I'LL BE

LADY.

> THERE I'LL BE

ALL WOMEN.

> THERE I'LL BE

> *(The* **LADIES** *have joined hands. A chime sounds.)*

LADY. Well, my dear, it's almost fifty years from the moment I first held you in my arms.

MARYANNE. Mom, this is really hard to say, but you were right. I want to thank all of you wonderful women for making this 49 year-old –

ALL. Ahem. *(etc.)*

MARYANNE. – You're right, this almost-FIFTY-year-old dog learn new tricks.

LADY. Happy birthday, Darling.

BARONESS. What do you wish for, MaryAnne?

PRINCESS. Yes, what do you wish?

MARYANNE. I wish for fifty more years of fun and friend-ship.

SONG: A BIG RED HAT

Lyrics by Amanda McBroom, Music by Michele Brourman

MARYANNE.

 I WILL LAUGH. I WILL CRY.
 I WILL DANCE WITHOUT ASKING WHY
 I WILL SING EVERY SONG THAT I HEAR IN MY HEAD
 I'LL WEAR MY HEART ON MY SLEEVE
 AND A HAT THAT'S RED.

 I WILL PAINT. I WILL WRITE.
 I WILL WATCH MY DREAMS TAKE FLIGHT
 I WILL SPEAK ALL THE WORDS I BELIEVE MUST BE
 SAID.
 WITH MY HEAD UP HIGH IN THE CLOUDS
 IN A HAT THAT'S RED.

 I'LL CLIMB THAT MOUNTAIN
 CROSS THE OCEAN
 FLY TO PARIS
 LEARN JAPANESE
 WITH SO MUCH OF MY LIFE YET TO EXPLORE,
 LET ME FLY THROUGH EACH OPENING DOOR.

 I WILL LEARN. I WILL TEACH
 I WILL HELP THOSE WITHIN MY REACH
 I WILL LOVE.

LADY & MARYANNE.

 AND WHAT ELSE COULD BE BETTER THAN THAT?

LADY, MARYANNE & BARONESS.

 WITH MY HEART ON MY SLEEVE

MARYANNE.

 MY HEAD IN THE CLOUDS

ALL LADIES.

 AND MY FRIENDS BY MY SIDE
 AND A BIG RED HAT

 ALL MY FRIENDS BY MY SIDE
 AND A BIG…RED…HAT!

 (*The girls applaud* **MARYANNE**. *She is finally one of them. All exit but* **MARYANNE** *and* **LADY**.)

MARYANNE. Mother, what are you doing?

LADY. I'm making a memory.

MARYANNE. A memory?

LADY. Yes, I want to remember this wonderful moment, because this is your passage, MaryAnne, your commencement to Fifty and Beyond. A memory is a picture you take with your heart.

(**LADY** *pulls a long feather out of* **MARYANNE**'s *red hat.*)

LADY. Do you know what this is?

MARYANNE. It looks like a quill pen.

LADY. Yes. It's to remind you not to abandon your dream. It's never too late. Write your story, MaryAnne. Even if it's just for you. *(She exits.)*

MARYANNE. OK, that got me. You made me cry, are you happy now? "Write your story even if it's just for you."

SONG: REPRISE A BIG RED HAT
Lyrics by Amanda McBroom, Music by Michele Brourman

MARYANNE.

> I WILL LEARN. I WILL TEACH
> I WILL HELP THOSE WITHIN MY REACH
> I WILL LOVE.
> AND WHAT ELSE COULD BE BETTER THAN THAT?
> WITH MY HEART ON MY SLEEVE
> MY HEAD IN THE CLOUDS
> AND MY FRIENDS BY MY SIDE
> AND A BIG RED HAT
> ALL MY FRIENDS BY MY SIDE
> AND A BIG...RED...HAT!

(She exits.)

SONG: PUT YOUR RED HAT ON
Lyrics by Susan Birkenhead, Music by Henry Krieger

(Throughout the MaryAnne's reprise, the women have changed from their regular clothes into fabulous over-the-top ensembles. The stage is now awash in sequin

and sparkle. Now it's **MARYANNE***'s turn to make the transformation.)*

LADY. *(spoken)* Sing it sister!!

DUCHESS.

PUT YOUR RED HAT ON,
AND YOU'LL FEEL LIKE A MILLION,
PUT YOUR RED HAT ON,
AND YOU'LL LOOK LIKE A STAR,

YOUR FEET START MOVIN',
YOUR HIPS START SWAYIN',
WHEREVER YOU GO, THERE'S MUSIC PLAYIN'

CONTESSA.	**GIRLS.**
PUT YOUR RED HAT ON AND THE WORLD WANTS TO KNOW YOU	PUT YOUR RED HAT ON KNOW YOU, KNOW YOU

BARONESS.	**GIRLS.**
PUT YOUR RED HAT ON AND YOU'LL LOVE WHO YOU ARE	PUT YOUR RED HAT ON AND YOU'LL LOVE WHO YOU ARE

LADY.

YOUR STEP IS LIGHTER,
YOUR WALK IS PROUDER,

DUCHESS.

YOUR HOPES AND DREAMS
ARE TALKIN' LOUDER

CONTESSA & BARONESS.	**GIRLS.**
PUT YOUR RED HAT ON PUT YOUR RED HAT ON	PUT YOUR RED HAT ON PUT YOUR RED HAT ON

ALL.

LIFE IS A PARTY.
YOU DON'T WANNA MISS.
LIFE IS A PORTERHOUSE STEAK.
LIFE IS A TANGO,
LIFE IS A KISS,
AND ALL OF THE NOISE YOU CAN MAKE.

(KEY CHANGE)

DAME.

>PUT YOUR RED HAT ON,
>WITH THE REST OF YOUR SISTERS

PRINCESS.

>PUT YOUR RED HAT ON,
>LET'S GO HAVE US SOME FUN,

ALL.

>IT'S ALL SO SIMPLE,
>NOTHIN' TO IT
>IT'S IN YOUR CLOSET,
>NOW GO AND DO IT

>PUT YOUR RED HAT ON

LADY, BARONESS, DAME.

>GO AND DO IT
>PUT YOUR RED HAT ON

PRINCESS, DUCHESS, CONTESSA.

>LIFE IS A PARTY

ALL.

>PUT YOUR RED HAT ON
>LET'S GO HAVE US SOME FUN

>PUT YOUR RED HAT, RED HAT...AH-AH-AHHHHN!!!

>**(MARYANNE** *enters from upstage center, dressed in her finale costume.)*

>PUT YOUR RED HAT ON,
>AND YOU'LL FEEL LIKE A MILLION
>PUT YOUR RED HAT ON,
>AND YOU'LL LOOK LIKE A STAR.

>IT'S ALL SO SIMPLE,
>NOTHIN' TO IT,
>IT'S IN YOUR CLOSET,
>NOW GO AND DO IT

>*(DOUBLE TIME GOSPEL:)*

>PUT YOUR RED HAT ON
>PUT YOUR RED HAT ON
>PUT YOUR RED HAT ON
>PUT YOUR RED HAT ON

PUT YOUR RED HAT ON
PUT YOUR RED HAT ON
PUT YOUR RED HAT ON
PUT YOUR RED HAT ON

PUT YOUR RED HAT
PUT YOUR RED HAT
PUT YOUR RED HAT…AH-AH-AHHHHN!!!

(Lights blackout to sillouhette.)

Curtain Call

COSTUME PLOT

Scene	MaryAnne	Duchess	Contessa	Baroness	Lady	Dame	Princess
FIFTY	Teal skirt Teal shell Teal blouse Turquoise necklace Tan heels	Dark brown slinky pants Gold crochet sweater Brown blouse Brown heels	Purple ruffled skirt Purple Beaded Sweater Red wedge heels	Red 2pc. Skirt suit Blue cowl neck red & black blouse Cream heels	Blue 2pc. Pant suit Blue cowl neck blouse Black strappy shoes	Green 2pc. Linen pantsuit Green silk floral shell Green flats	Orange linen pants Orange linen shell w/beads Orange & green burnout blouse Tan char. Shoes
I DON'T WANT	same						
Duchess/Contessa	same	same	Striped blouse Striped skirt *Red wedge heels				
CINCO PASSOS	same	Black slinky pants Red & gold stretch shell Red floral tie-front blouse Black charactyer shoes Feathered "Carmen Miranda" hat	Striped ruffled skirt Red & gold stretch blouse *Red front blouse Black wedge heels Fancy character shoes Feathered "Carmen Miranda" hat	Black slinky pants Red & gold stretch shell Red floral tie-front blouse Black character shoes Feathered "Carmen Miranda" hat	Black slinky pants Red & gold stretch shell Red floral tie-front blouse Black character shoes Feathered "Carmen Miranda" hat	Black slinky pants Red & gold stretch shell Red floral tie-front blouse Black character shoes Feathered "Carmen Miranda" hat	Black slinky pants Red & gold stretch shell Red floral tie-front blouse Black character shoes Feathered "Carmen Miranda" hat
Baroness Monologue/All Work & No Play	same			Red skirt suit Black tank Cream heels			
OLDER THE FIDDLE	same	Black slinky pantsRed & gold stretch shell Black & white cow vest Black character shoes Red straw cowboy hat		Red skirt suit Black tank Cream Heels Red felt cowboy hat w/feather	Blue pants Blue cowl neck blouse Black strappy heels Black and white cow vest Red straw cowboy hat	Black slinky pantsRed & gold stretch shell Black & white cow vest Black character shoes Red straw cowboy hat	Black slinky pantsRed & gold stretch shell Black & white cow vest Red character shoes Red straw cowboy hat

Scene	MaryAnne	Duchess	Contessa	Baroness	Lady	Dame	Princess
CELEBRATE					Blue pants Blue cowl neck blouse Black strappy heels Black and white cow vest Red straw cowboy hat		
Baroness Speech 2/Dating Again	same			Red skirt suit Black tank Cream Heels	Blue pants Blue cowl neck blouse Black strappy heels		
MY EMPTY NEST						Green linen pants Green silk floral shell Green embroidered blouse Red "My Fair Lady" hat w/flowers	
Baroness Crossover				Professional attire			
JUST LIKE ME							Black slinky pants Black tank Black character shoes Trench coat Blue silk scarf
			Black slinky pants Black tank Cream satin blouse Black character shoes Black fedora w/sequin band Sparkly belt	Black slinky pants Black tank Cream satin blouse Black character shoes Black fedora w/sequin band Sparkly belt	Black slinky pants Black tank Cream satin blouse Black character shoes Black fedora w/sequin band Sparkly belt	Black slinky pants Black tank Cream satin blouse Black character shoes Black fedora w/sequin band Sparkly belt	
Quotes Corner	same	Black velvet skirt Black sheer jacket w/silver sequins Black shell w/silver glitter Lucite heels w/rhinestones White fedora w/sequin band					
MY OVEN'S STILL HOT	same			same		same	

Scene	MaryAnne	Duchess	Contessa	Baroness	Lady	Dame	Princess
Princess & MaryAnne Heart to Heart	same						Orange linen pants Orange linen shell w/beads Orange & green burnout blouse Tan char. Shoes
Lady & Dame Yarn					Black slinky pants character shoes Blue cowl neck blouse Black Green socks Green fleece character shoes Blue robe Yellow roller fleece robe Blue socks Pink roller hat hat Granny glasses	Black slinky pants Green linen shell Green linen jacket Black character shoes	
YES WE CAN (golf)		Brown slinky pants Gold crochet sweater Brown heels			same	same	Orange linen pants Orange knit shell Orange floral burnout shirt Tan character shoes Red golf glove Red visor
YES WE CAN (yoga)			Striped blouse Striped skirt Red wedge sandals	Black slinky pants Red stretch shell Black character shoes	same	same	Orange linen pants Orange knit shell Orange floral burnout shirt Tan character shoes
YES WE CAN (tap dance)	Black slinky pants Teal shell Teal blouse Black character shoes	Black slinky pants Gold crochet sweater Black character shoes	Black slinky pants Purple beaded sweater Black character shoes	same	same	same	Orange linen pants Orange knit shell Orange floral burnout shirt Tan character shoes Orange hair band
YES WE CAN (can-can)	same				same	Black slinky pants Green linen shell Green linen jacket Black character shoes	same

Scene	MaryAnne	Duchess	Contessa	Baroness	Lady	Dame	Princess
Shopping		Black sheer beaded jacket Black stretch pants Black long line bra Black marabou sandals		Pink horror dress w/security tag	same	same	
FIDDLE (REPRISE)		Brown slinky pants Gold crochet top Brown heels		Red pretty dress Cream heels	same	same	
Princess Monologue	Teal skirt Teal shell teal blouse Tan shoes						Orange linen pants Orange knit shell Orange floral burnout shirt Tan character shoes Red pillbox hat
INVISIBLE	Teal skirt Teal shell Teal blouse Turquoise necklace Tan heels	Brown slinky pants Gold crochet top Brown shirt Brown heels	Purple ruffled skirt Purple Beaded Sweater Red wedge heels	Red 2pc. Skirt suit Red & black blouse Cream heels	Blue pantsuit Blue cowl neck blouse Black strappy shoes	Green linen pants Green silk floral shell Green embroidered shirt Green flats	same
A BIG RED HAT	Teal skirt Teal shell Teal blouse Turquoise necklace Tan heels Red & purple hat w/feather	same	same	same	same	same	same
A BIG RED HAT (REPRISE)	same						
PUT YOUR RED HAT ON	Purple sparkly wrap dress w/rose petal trim Red hat w/flower petals Red heels Red gloves w/clear sequins	Deep purple spaghetti-strap jumpsuit Sheer jacket Red hat w/purple feather Red short gloves Red shoes w/sequined toes	Red and purple flouncy wrap dress Red short gloves Red feathered headdress Red wedge heels	Purple cowgirl jumpsuit Purple bolero jacket Red cowboy boots Red gloves w/ beaded fringe Red cowboy hat w/silver "studs"	Purple and red chiffon dress Red floppy straw hat with sequins Red elbow/length gloves Red slip-on sandals	Purple chiffon & sequin dress Giant red "tutu" Red elbow-length gloves Red sandals w/gold circle Purple feather boa	Purple dress w/ 12in. Red fringe Red strappy sandals Red opera-length gloves Red feather boa Red sequined pillbox hat

THE RED HAT SOCIETY is a network of women from all walks of life dedicated to showing the world that there is fun after fifty. Its mission is to gain higher visibility for women and to reshape the way they are viewed by today's culture. Formed eight years ago, Red Hat Society currently has more than 40,000 chapters in all 50 states, and more than 30 countries, creating a world-wide sisterhood intent on touching and enriching the lives of its members. Becoming a member of The Red Hat Society is fun, fast and easy. For more information on the Red Hat Society, visit www.redhatsociety.com. Members can also sign up for Purple Perks to receive discounts to over 50,000 venues across North America.

From the Reviews of
HATS!...

"If you want to see something really magnificent, not just a great musical, but a magnificent presence, go see *Hats!*"
- Whoopi Goldberg, Wake up With Whoopi

"That's a real audience emitting real belly laughs and crying real tears...I have never seen an audience so affected in the course of watching theater."
- John Moore, *The Denver Post*

"This is a feel-good show that's really about feeling good!...Its high spirits perpetually come through."
- Steven Oxman, *Variety*

"The entirely original collection of musical numbers about being fifty and fabulous were penned by some of Broadway and Cabaret's brightest lights, including Henry Krieger ('Dreamgirls'), Carol Hall ('The Best Little Whorehouse in Texas') and Amanda McBroom ('The Rose'). Unsurprising then, many of these numbers are melodic, insightful and easy on the ear."
- Chris Jones, *Chicago Tribune*

Women of the Red Hat Society exclaim:

"*Hats!* Is marvelous, hilarious, tear-jerking, riotous, wonderful. If we weren't laughing, we were crying or clapping...I can't write enough superlatives to do it justice. Just wonderful."
- Judy of the Red Hat Chapter, The Blackfoot Babes

Breinigsville, PA USA
31 January 2010
231647BV00005B/1/P